Fairies
in Spring Flowers

Written and Illustrated by
Lisa R Davis

Dedicated to Mark, my husband and best friend

Also by Lisa R Davis
Fairies In My Flowerbeds

ISBN-13: 978-1493593064
ISBN-10: 1493593064

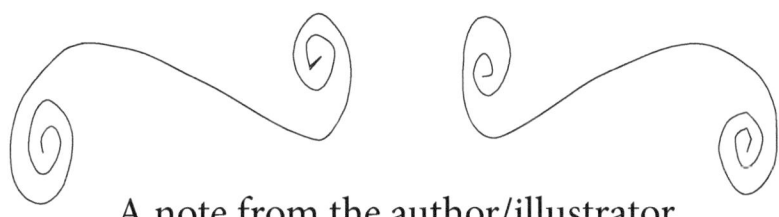

A note from the author/illustrator

Once upon a spring while tending her flowers, a gardener started seeing things she had never seen before. Tiny whimsical heads seemed to be peeking at her, as if they were trying to draw attention. Little figures clothed in fanciful dresses of blossoms with soft petal wings appeared before her eyes...

That gardener was me. I had never seen a fairy before, but going on hearsay and the art of others, I decided what I was seeing must be fairies. I was surprised and amazed as the figures took form, and as each of their personalities began to shine. They inspired me.

This book contains images of some of the fairies that populate my spring gardens. They don't have mouths, so they never talk to me, but many times it feels as if they speak directly to my heart.

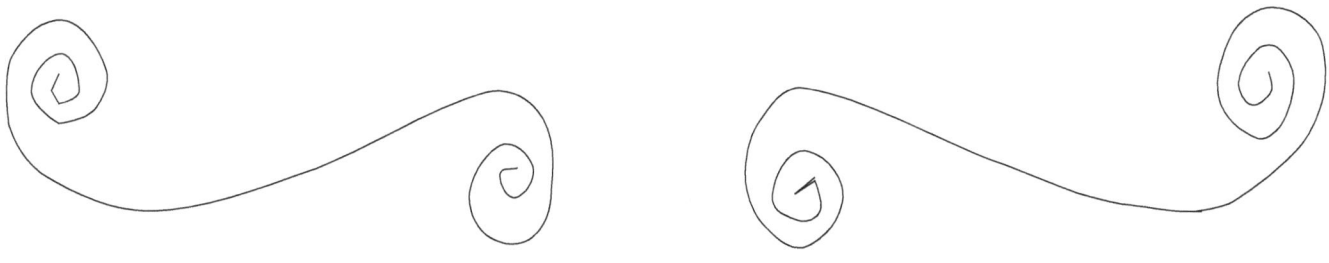

My special thanks to Joe Abbate, Mark Davis, Jim Farfaglia, Debbie Hough, and Diane Sokolowski. With their keen and critical eyes, they push me—in the kindest, gentlest ways—to continue to improve and grow.

They're Coming!

It may still be cold outside
but spring is in the air;
if you pay close attention,
the signs are everywhere.

Though snowflakes still drift about,
the ground is growing bare.
See those dangling snowdrops
that are blooming over there...

And here's a stretching crocus;
what joy has filled my day,
for that means springtime fairies
will now come out to play!

1

Meet the Snowdrops

At first I just saw flowers
but then at second glance,
I also spied two fairies
and did a happy dance.

Both were dressed quite warmly
in sweaters white like snow,
with matching hats to keep them snug
in case cold winds did blow.

Though it was way too chilly
to stay outside for long,
because I'd seen them playing,
I sang a cheerful song.

Fairies:
sweaters, heads and hats: snowdrop blossoms
wings: crocus petals
skirt: a crocus blossom
legs: crocus leaves

Flowers:
Crocus tommasinianus
common names: early crocus, woodland crocus,
snow crocus, or tommies
Galanthus nivalis
common name: snowdrop

3

Eli
Crocus

Since most plants still are sleeping
this early in the year,
it seems to me like magic
when these suddenly appear.

This energetic fairy-boy
looked like a bumblebee,
inspecting recent garden growth,
flying, wild and free.

Because it was still frosty out,
his cheeks were red and rosy,
but his smart cap with yellow fringe
helped keep him warm and cozy.

Fairy:
hat: a coltsfoot blossom with sepals
coat: a crocus bud
legs and arms: crocus leaves
wings: wild strawberry leaves

Flowers:
Tussilago farfara
common names: coltsfoot, hallfoot, horsehoof,
foalswort, fieldhove, bullsfoot, donnhove

Lucy Snow

Glory-of-the-snow they're called,
petals all aglow,
looking like blue fallen stars
against soft drifts of snow.

Lucy's in her glory
during frosty new spring days,
but alas, she'll have to change her clothes
when sunshine starts to blaze.

As days grow long and nights get short
those blue stars disappear;
they will not be seen again
till early spring next year.

Fairy:
dress: a glory-of-the-snow blossom
head and hat: a primrose bud with sepals
wings: partridgeberry leaves
legs and arms: glory-of-the-snow leaves and stems

Flowers:
Chionodoxa lucililiae
common names: glory-of-the-snow,
Lucille's glory-of-the-snow

7

Constance Crocus

The weather can't make up its mind
this fickle time of year,
but Constance never worries,
for she wears her special gear.

On those March and April days
so overcast and cold,
she'll snuggle up and stay quite warm
inside her cape of gold.

She'll open it up widely
when the sun shines warm and bright,
but if the chill and clouds return,
she's sure to close it tight.

Fairy:
dress and cape: a crocus blossom
wings: crocus petals
arms and legs: crocus leaves
head: a primrose bud with sepals

Flowers:
Crocus chrysanthus
common name: snow crocus

9

Amelia Primrose

In her shawl and pointed hat
she's such a charming sight,
adding color to spring gardens
with her blushing face, so bright.

She's also quite the fashion plate
decked out in mini skirt,
but you will only see her
when you're quiet and alert.

For at times she wraps her wings
to make a place to hide;
when you see a crocus folded up,
she could be tucked inside.

Fairy:

dress and arms: an opening primrose blossom with sepals

head and hat: a primrose bud with sepals

wings: crocus petals

legs: crocus leaves

Flowers:
Primula vulgaris
common names: primrose,
common primrose, English primrose

11

Diana Daffodil

In the fall, dry bulbs are nestled
underneath the ground.
Six months later, up they sprout,
for spring has rolled around.

They brighten up my flowerbeds,
but I received an added thrill—
a fairy sporting crocus wings
dressed in a glowing daffodil.

With matching garden gloves and boots
to protect her hands and feet,
she's busy tending sprouting plants
to keep them looking neat.

Fairy:
dress: an opening daffodil blossom with sepal
hands and feet: grape hyacinths
wings: crocus petals
head: nigella seedpod
hat: the inner part (carona) of a daffodil blossom

Flowers:
Narcissus
common name: daffodil
Muscari neglectum
common name: grape hyacinth

13

Miss Pansy and the Viola Sisters

Each spring I get excited
when I see this group arrive.
These fairies like cool weather;
indeed, that's why they thrive.

The big one seems a shepherdess
but she doesn't safeguard sheep.
She tends wee fairies all day long
then tucks them in to sleep.

If they begin to wander off,
she has a special trick—
she softly draws them back to her
with her fancy walking stick.

Fairies:

Miss Pansy:

dress and arms: a pansy blossom

wings: pansy petals

head and hat: a pansy bud

legs: pansy stems

The Viola Sisters:

gowns and arms: opening viola blossoms

with sepals

wings: viola petals

heads: single grape hyacinth blossoms

Flowers:
Viola x *wittrockiana*
common name: pansy

Leah Trillium

The woods in spring are magical,
with changes everyday.
When entering a peaceful glade
my cares just fall away.

Listen for the songs of birds
and see what you can spy.
One fine day you just might see
this pixie passing by.

She, along with fairy kin,
gather in April and May,
to play games 'neath budded trees—
like Pixieland croquet.

Fairy:

dress and arms: a white trillium flower with sepals

head: a red trillium bud with sepals

wings: trillium leaves

legs: crocus leaves

mallet: a tendril

ball: winterberry

Flower:
Trillium gandiflorum
common names: white trillium,
white wake-robin

Addie

A Lily of the Woods

Clumps of pointed, mottled leaves
sprout from the forest floor,
then up come star-like flowers
that I really do adore.

Among a group of forest blooms
which warming sunshine brings,
I found this woodland fairy-girl
with lovely dappled wings.

She wears a rice hat on her head
but she's not from Japan.
Addie's from the USA—
it is her native land.

Fairy:
dress: an adder's tongue blossom
wings: adder's tongue leaves
head: a partridge berry
hat: a rolled partridge berry leaf
arms and legs: adder's tongue stems

Flowers:
Erythronium americanum
common names: adder's tongue, trout lily, fawn lily,
yellow dog-toothed violet, and yellow snowdrop

19

Wendy Windflower

Windflowers will fold up at night
and in folklore it's said
that sleepy fairies slip inside
to snuggle into bed.

This fairy wasn't tired—
what she wanted was a wrap—
with a frilly, silly bonnet
and matching wings to flap.

She had electric energy
and beckoned me to play;
we frolicked in the garden,
keeping warm one chilly day.

Fairy:
dress: a Grecian windflower blossom
wings and hat: Grecian windflower leaves
head: snowdrop anemone
arms and legs: Grecian windflower stems

Flower:
Anemone blanda
common names: Grecian windflower,
winter windflower or sapphire anemone

21

Silas Tulip-Daffodil

A tulip or a daffodil—
he couldn't choose just one;
he finds both intriguing—
their colors, fire and sun.

He warms up cool spring gardens,
festive and so bright,
craving technicolors
after winter's frigid white.

He basks in sultry sunshine
and drinks up cool spring rains.
He leaves before the summer comes
but in my heart, remains.

Fairy:
cloak: a tulip blossom
wings: tulip and daffodil petals
head: a daffodil seedpod
hat: the center part (corona) of a daffodil blossom
arms and legs, hands and feet: daffodil stems with undeveloped seedpod tips

Flowers:
Narcissus
common name: daffodil
Tulipa
common name: tulip

The Royal Raja Leaf Bud

He looked like Indian royalty
with a turban on his head,
different from the others—
not of a flower bed.

The size of a large bumble bee,
an active, striking fellow,
with a handsome little beard,
fuzzy, soft and yellow.

Clothed in robes of palest green,
sprinkled with white fur,
while parading through my yard,
he created quite a stir.

Fairy:
body, head, arms and turban: a single maple leaf bud
wings: the leaves of a maple tree seedling

Twig with foliage:
Acer
common name: maple tree

25

Maggie Magnolia

An apron tied around her waist,
a kerchief on her head,
she looks like she could be a maid
or maybe baking bread.

But looks can be deceiving;
what a big surprise for me,
to discover who Miss Maggie is—
turn the page to see...

Fairy:
dress and arms: a saucer magnolia blossom with leaf buds
wings: tulip petals
head: a magnolia bud and leaflets

Flower:
Magnolia × soulangeana
common name: saucer magnolia

27

Lady Magnolia

This is the same sweet Maggie—
with changed wings and new hairstyle,
and fancy shoes upon her feet;
she's very versatile.

She is an aristocrat
with a title to her name,
but though now she's all dressed up,
inside she's still same.

She wanted to look special
for an elegant affair;
with the garden for her closet,
this is what she chose to wear.

Fairy:

dress and arms: a saucer magnolia blossom with leaf buds

wings: tulip petals

head: an uncapped acorn

shoes: fringed leaf bleeding heart blossoms

hair: a bleeding heart blossom, split in half

Flower:
Tulipa
common name: tulip

29

Starr and Stella Magnolia

The star magnolia is a shrub,
or even a small tree,
growing graceful, gleaming flowers,
a lovely sight to see.

Flying 'round this giant bush
I found two charming fairies.
Dressed and airborne as they were,
they looked like white canaries.

I think these girls were sisters,
though they weren't alike at all,
for Starr was short and lively,
and Stella, calm and tall.

Fairies:

Starr:

dress and arms: a star magnolia blossom with leaf buds

wings: tulip petals

head: a daffodil seedpod

hat: a hyacinth blossom

legs and shoes: phlox buds with stems

Stella:

dress and arms: a star magnolia blossom with leaf buds

wings: white daffodil petals

head: a star magnolia bud

legs: crocus leaves

carrying a fringed leaf bleeding heart

Flower: *Magnolia stellata* — common name: star magnolia

Friendly Finley Tulip

She waved to me becomingly
as I was bustling by.
I was in a hurry,
though I don't remember why.

She was so enticing
that I had to stop and play,
for cavorting with a fairy-girl
doesn't happen everyday.

If you ever get the chance
to spend the day with one,
make the time, it'll be worthwhile—
you won't forget the fun!

Fairy:
jumper: a columbine blossom
wings: petals from two different tulips
blouse: a bleeding heart blossom
head and hair: a chive bud
arms and legs: chive stems

Flowers: *Dicentra spectabilis*—common
name: bleeding heart
Tulipa—common name: tulip

33

Marcy and Merlin May Apple

Some call them umbrella plants,
but the most amazing sight
is what these plantings look like
when their leaves are rolled up tight...

It's a fairy congregation
rising from the forest floor;
they huddle, sharing secrets,
every spring since days of yore.

They gather by the hundreds,
but when it gets too warm,
they open up their brown cloaks
and green umbrellas form!

Fairies:
heads, cloaks and legs: furled Mayapple leaves, buds, and stems
wings: trillium leaves

Plant:
Podophyllum peltatum
common names: Mayapple or May apple, umbrella plant, hogapple, Indian apple, mayflower, wild lemon, wild mandrake, American mandrake, may pop, devil's apple, racoon berry, duck's foot

Adam Azalea

I saw a fairy-baby,
a glowing, friendly sprout,
romping in my shrubbery
while swooping all about.

It took some time to spot him
for he capered in the shade;
I loved his sunset colors
and the carefree way he played.

He showed off with somersaults,
then backflips through the air;
his fine acrobatics were
accomplished with great flair!

Fairy:
gown: an azalea blossom and bud
wings: flowering quince petals
head: a squill seedpod
hat: a primrose calyx

Flower:
Rhododendron subgenus *Pentanthera*
common name: azalea

37

Fancy Foxglove

Have you ever seen a foxglove gown?
I hope you'll answer, "yes,"
for this fairy's wearing one—
her lovely, long white dress.

Chosen specially by her;
she loved the way it fit,
but insisted on bright colors
for wings to flap and flit.

As for that tall, purple hat,
it's not one I would wear,
but she picked it for herself,
and in it, looks most fair!

Fairy:

dress and vest: a foxglove blossom with calyx

head: a myrtle spurge seedpod

hat: a penstemon blossom

arms and legs: columbine seedpods

wings: climbing rose petals

Flower:
Digitalis purpurea
common name: foxglove

39

Open Eyes

Spring fairies come together
before they take their leave,
for time is passing quickly,
and now it's summer's eve.

This parting's not forever;
they'll all return next year.
Until then, you can visit them
in the pages you have here.

I'd like to give you some advice:
look around when you're outside,
for you'll notice wondrous things
when your eyes are open wide.

41

A note about the illustrations

The illustrations in this book were created using a technique called scanography, which can also be called scanner art or scanner photography. Instead of using a camera to capture an image, a scanographer uses a flatbed scanner. First, I gathered pieces and parts of my garden flowers and the plants that surround my country home, and then arranged those materials face down on my scanner. After doing multiple previews, rearranging the plant parts each time, I obtained an image that "spoke" to me. Those images were refined and completed in a graphic arts program.

One of my spring gardens

For more pictures of my gardens, to see more fairies, or to contact me,
visit my website:
www.WallflowersAndCards.com

www.ingramcontent.com/pod-product-compliance
Lightning Source LLC
Chambersburg PA
CBHW041520280526
45792CB00004B/1315